The Bears Sleep at Last

BY GENEVIÈVE BILLETTE

TRANSLATED BY NADINE DESROCHERS

PLAYWRIGHTS CANADA PRESS
TORONTO

LIBRARY AND ARCHIVES CANADA CATALOGUING IN PUBLICATION
Title: The bears sleep at last / by Geneviève Billette ; translated by Nadine Desrochers.
Other titles: Ours dorment enfin. English
Names: Billette, Geneviève, author. | Desrochers, Nadine, 1971- translator.
Description: First English edition. | A play. | Translation of: Les ours dorment enfin.
Identifiers: Canadiana (print) 20190082526 | Canadiana (ebook)
20190082534 | ISBN 9781770919952 (softcover) | ISBN 9780369100030 (PDF)
| ISBN 9780369100047 (EPUB) | ISBN 9780369100054 (Kindle)
Classification: LCC PS8553.I4395 O8713 2019 | DDC C842/.54—dc23

Playwrights Canada Press acknowledges that we operate on land, which, for thousands of years, has been the traditional territories of the Mississaugas of the Credit First Nation, Huron-Wendat, Anishinaabe, Métis, and Haudenosaunee peoples. Today, this meeting place is home to many Indigenous peoples from across Turtle Island and we are grateful to have the opportunity to work and play here.

We acknowledge the financial support of the Government of Canada through the National Translation Program for Book Publishing, an initiative of the *Roadmap for Canada's Official Languages 2013–2018: Education, Immigration, Communities*, for our translation activities, and the Canada Council for the Arts—which last year invested $153 million to bring the arts to Canadians throughout the country—the Ontario Arts Council (OAC), Ontario Creates, and the Government of Canada for our publishing activities.

ONTARIO ARTS COUNCIL
CONSEIL DES ARTS DE L'ONTARIO
an Ontario government agency
un organisme du gouvernement de l'Ontario

To little Sasha (who is quite real).

Les ours dorment enfin was first produced in
December 2011 by L'Eldorado Théâtre with Théâtre
Bouches Décousues at Théâtre de la Ville in
Longueuil, Québec, with the following cast and
creative team:

Vincent Magnat
Sébastien René

Director: Stéphanie Lépine
Assistant Director: Marie-Christine Martel
Set Design: Geneviève Lizotte
Assisstant Set Design: Valérie Archambault
Sound Design: Eric Shaw
Lighting Design: Anne-Marie Rodrigue Lecours
Costume Design: Sophie Limoges
Technical Director: Jérémi Guilbault Asselin
Stage Manager: Marjorie Bélanger
Creative Consultant: Benoît Vermeulen

THE CHARACTERS

Sasha
Marcus
. . . and three bears(*)

(*) In the author's mind, these should not be puppets. These bears should only appear as a collective motion, and their appearance could perhaps be inspired by visual arts. But she leaves it up to the directors' imaginations to find the best solutions in light of their artistic projects.

THE LOCATIONS

Sasha's apartment
The bears' cage

SASHA's *apartment. Clearly displayed, an enormous calendar. A date is circled in thick red ink.* SASHA *enters in a rush.* MARCUS *runs to him.* SASHA *hurriedly begins to make* MARCUS's *bed.*

MARCUS: Did the ice work?

SASHA: Almost.

MARCUS: Did they yawn? Did they bat their eyelids?

SASHA: Not yet, but I have hope. I've just received the first delivery. I never would have thought that ice would be so heavy to transport. That being said, those blocks are enormous . . .

MARCUS: Sir . . . do you think it's my fault?

SASHA: What?

MARCUS: That the bears are not sleeping?

SASHA: Why would it be your fault?

MARCUS: I always have the feeling that everything's my fault.

SASHA: It's winter's fault, Marcus. It's winter's fault for being late. The bears need the cold of winter to fall asleep. Mid-January! And you would swear this warmth is autumnal. Temperatures should have dropped weeks ago. They should have been asleep weeks ago.

MARCUS: They must be tired . . .

. . .

SASHA: They look like ghosts. They breathe slowly, their hearts have slowed their pace. Even hunger has left them . . . Their whole bodies are ready for sleep, but sleep doesn't come. They walk around in circles, eyes wide open.

MARCUS: Do you think they're suffering?

SASHA: I have never seen such a look in their eyes. Come on, off to bed.

MARCUS: Sir . . . are you really sure it's not my fault?

SASHA: I said so, didn't I?

MARCUS: Then why aren't you making your bed next to mine, like yesterday? That's a bad sign.

SASHA: I have to go back to the zoo, Marcus. Tons of ice blocks are waiting for me. I would like to get my bears to sleep tonight.

MARCUS: In a way, it's a big bed of ice that you will make for them.

SASHA: You could say that.

MARCUS: You made my bed. You go make the bears' bed. Then you come back to make yours . . . next to mine.

SASHA: Deal. I'm off before the ice melts. The ice!

SASHA runs to his bag. He takes out a piece of ice, already liquefying, and hands it to MARCUS.

Quick, take it, it's for you . . . Come on, take it!

MARCUS: It's . . . it's a very nice gift, sir.

SASHA: Quick! Go to a corner of the apartment where you feel good and rub the ice on your bum.

MARCUS doesn't react.

Don't be shy, I won't look. It will be cold, but it will make you feel better. It's not normal for a bum to be blue.

MARCUS: You can give it to the bears, sir.

SASHA: I took the smallest piece. This one is for you. Hurry! It's already melting.

MARCUS: My bum is not blue anymore.

SASHA: What?

MARCUS: I waited for you all day. You don't even have a TV. I had nothing else to do but look at my bum. It's not blue anymore.

SASHA: You're sure?

MARCUS: I looked at it every hour on the hour. Pink at nine o'clock, pink at noon, pink still when the sun went down.

SASHA: It doesn't hurt anymore?

MARCUS: Not at all. I was healed in one day!

SASHA: That's true—it's incredible, you only just got here yesterday . . .

MARCUS: Did it seem longer to you? That's also a bad sign, sir.

SASHA: I'm just a little lost in time, that's all. Actually, it's more like time is toying with me.

MARCUS: You should have written the date of my arrival on the calendar. That's what people do with important events . . . if I'm an important event for you.

SASHA: You can say that again.

MARCUS: Oh!

SASHA: But I never write anything on the calendar.

MARCUS: There is a date that's circled. In red.

SASHA: I circled it, and I will not circle any other.

MARCUS: Why?

SASHA: Because.

MARCUS: Got it, sir, it's none of my business.

SASHA: Marcus, I've got an idea. What if, to celebrate your recovery, you stopped calling me "sir"?

MARCUS: You don't like it? I thought it sounded polite, that you thought, "Oh, this boy is as refined as sugar . . . " That with each "sir" I earned more points.

SASHA: Every time you say it, for a second I wonder who you're talking to.

MARCUS: Nobody calls you "sir"?

SASHA: I work with bears, Marcus. They are not so formal.

MARCUS: How would you like me to address you?

SASHA: You could try using my name . . .

MARCUS: That would make sense.

SASHA extends a hand towards MARCUS.

SASHA: Good night, Marcus.

MARCUS: Good night, Sasha.

SASHA's *apartment.* MARCUS *wakes with a start in the middle of the night. He talks, rapidly, to escape the nightmare.*

MARCUS: Sasha! I dreamt nothing had stuck, that my hands, on the glass of your window, my hands, they hadn't stuck because the glass was too wet, nothing had stuck, you hadn't seen me, I was falling, falling, you hadn't seen me! Sasha? Sasha?!

SASHA's apartment. SASHA enters, looking rough: he has not slept a wink. MARCUS rushes to meet him.

MARCUS: So?

SASHA: Nothing.

MARCUS: Not even a yawn?

SASHA: Not yet.

MARCUS: Are you sure the ice was really cold?

SASHA: Ice is always cold, Marcus.

MARCUS: Yes, but maybe you didn't work fast enough, maybe the ice had time to melt . . . Nobody can fall asleep in a wet bed.

. . .

SASHA: You're probably right. At least it made them feel better.

MARCUS: You think so?

SASHA: I felt it right away. You know, Marcus, the bears and I, we are . . . connected, like brothers. I know everything about them—they know everything about me. We can't hide anything from one another.

I'm sorry I couldn't be here last night. I hope you weren't scared?

MARCUS: Not at all. I had the most wonderful dream.

SASHA: That's nice.

MARCUS: What are you going to do?

SASHA: Sleep for a while, then start again. Faster, this time. I can't stop at making them feel better. I want to give them back their slumber.

MARCUS: Have you thought of telling them a story?

SASHA: I talk to them all the time.

MARCUS: Yes, but an actual story . . . Maybe that would help them fall asleep?

SASHA: I don't know any.

MARCUS: There's nothing inside your head that begins with, "Once upon a time . . . "?

SASHA: I don't feel like stirring up memories.

MARCUS: Why?

SASHA: I don't feel like it, that's all.

MARCUS: Take a story that's very close. Tonight, you could practise by telling it to me . . .

SASHA: Marcus, were you scared last night?

MARCUS: Not at all.

SASHA: Are you sure?

MARCUS: Even if I was lying . . . I feel good, here, Sasha. Here, with you, is the best I've ever felt.

4

The zoo, at night. The bears wander heavily. Only SASHA
*is lit. Without respite, he lays blocks of ice, preceding the
bears' footsteps as though rolling out a carpet. The work
is gruelling.* SASHA *stops to catch his breath as the bears
continue their aimless walk.*

SASHA: What if I tried? No, that's ridiculous. And why not, just
to catch my breath?

(to the bears) My sweethearts, my furry darlings . . . I can't promise
I'll be spellbinding, but . . . I will . . . I will tell you a story.

The bears stop walking and turn towards SASHA.

Here we go. Once upon a time . . . or rather, a morning . . . a
morning not at all far away, I was having a quiet breakfast, bagel
and scrambled eggs, when all of a sudden, "Bam!" A mighty blow
against the window. I live on the third floor, it had to be a bird . . .
I wasn't in the mood, that morning, for a bird to be hurt. I didn't
have the heart to run down the stairs and take in a wounded

bird. It was enough to worry about you, and besides, wounded birds never heal. I turned my head, slowly, dreading the vastness of the bloody stain on the glass . . . That's when I saw the most incredible thing.

> *MARCUS appears, his face flat against a pane of glass. His hands are spread apart but his feet are touching, and all are stuck to the glass. SASHA slowly approaches.*

What on earth is that?

(to the bears) My whole being wanted to just shut the curtains.

> *MARCUS's mouth is stuck to the glass. He speaks, but his words are incomprehensible.*

What?

> *MARCUS speaks again.*

I don't understand.

> *Smack! MARCUS "de-suctions" himself from the window.*

MARCUS: Sir, sir, can you hear me?

SASHA: Ehm . . . like through a pane of glass. But yes, I can hear you.

MARCUS: If you only knew how happy I am, sir. I have tried to stick myself to so many windows, at least six, maybe ten. It wouldn't stick. It never stuck. Either the curtains would close or my hands got scared, then wet, and I would slide down. Here, it seems to stick for sure.

SASHA: How did you do it?

MARCUS: I don't know.

SASHA: Scientifically, it's impossible.

MARCUS: If you say so, then I agree.

SASHA: To get to someone's home on the third floor, you climb the stairs. Then you ring the bell. But to arrive as though in flight and smash your nose on the window . . .

MARCUS: It's not polite?

SASHA: It's impossible.

MARCUS: You should tell that to the wind. It does whatever it wants with me.

SASHA: Even if the wind had lifted you up . . . All matter gravitates towards the ground. If you throw a pebble in the air, what does it do?

MARCUS: With my luck, it falls on my head. Same thing when I spit.

SASHA: You see, you say so yourself: everything falls back down.

MARCUS: But, sir, I too have always fallen back down. If that's what's worrying you . . .

SASHA: Yet this time, you are not falling. How are you doing that?

MARCUS: I don't know. This is the first time it sticks. I told you, sir, yours is perhaps the tenth window I have tried to cling on to. Each time I would slide down and fall. You don't have to worry, I am quite normal—I always ended up falling. Just to show you how normal I am: my bum is blue.

SASHA: Your bum is blue?

MARCUS: Because of having fallen so many times. My bad luck, as always. It landed me on concrete more often than on tulip beds. And so, my bum is blue.

SASHA: That must hurt terribly . . .

MARCUS: Say, sir, would you mind unsticking me?

SASHA: Unsticking you . . . ?

MARCUS: If you prefer, come and pick me, like an apple. I don't know how to say or do it—this is the first time it's stuck.

SASHA: I don't know either . . .

MARCUS: I don't want to sound impolite, sir, and I do enjoy chatting with you, but it would be nice if you could hurry. If it were to unstick again . . . my bum couldn't take it. Even though it's January, all I see on the ground is good, solid concrete, not snow.

SASHA: *(to the bears)* I ran down the stairs of the building. I grabbed the superintendent's ladder.

MARCUS: Hurry, sir. My left hand . . . it's not sticking anymore!

SASHA: I climbed up to him.

SASHA positions himself behind MARCUS, who is still glued to the window. SASHA begins to open his arms, but stops mid-motion.

Yet something held me back.

MARCUS: My feet are unsticking too!

SASHA hesitates for one second . . . then two . . . then three . . .

Please, sir.

SASHA hesitates still.

I am only holding on with one hand!

SASHA is still hesitating. He finally makes up his mind. With one swift and sharp motion, he grabs hold of MARCUS.

If you only knew how happy I am, sir!

MARCUS disappears.

SASHA: *(to the bears)* I carried him up to my place. As quickly as he had hit my window, he fell asleep. I still didn't understand. I waited until, in his sleep, he turned onto his stomach. Then, very gently, I pulled up his sweater. The shoulders were normal, under the shoulders, the shoulder blades were also normal . . . I think seeing feathers would have reassured me. No, a nice smooth back. No trace of anything even remotely resembling feathers. Despite that, he had flown to me. And from that very second, I wanted to have him in my life.

That was the end of my story.

The bears start walking again.

Poor Sasha . . . How could you hope a story would put them to sleep . . .

He gets back to work.

Hang in there, my sweethearts, hang in there, my furry darlings. Winter cannot have deserted us forever. No, not forever.

5

SASHA's *apartment. They are sitting at the table. In fact, only* MARCUS *is eating, but with visible pleasure.* SASHA *seems quite distracted.*

MARCUS: I've never had anything so good . . .

SASHA: . . .

MARCUS: Really, it's just so good. What is it?

SASHA: . . .

MARCUS: This is awkward. I'm almost done and your plate is still full. Maybe I'll steal a bite . . .

SASHA *still doesn't react;* MARCUS *steals a bit of meat from* SASHA's *plate.*

Mmmmmm . . . Maybe I'll steal another . . .

He does.

Maybe I'll put my finger in your sauce . . .

He does.

If there is room for one, there might be room for two.

He adds another finger. SASHA *still doesn't react.*

Away with formality and into the deep end.

He puts his entire hand in the sauce, making it splash around.

Sasha, tell your hand to join mine—the sauce is perfect for a swim!

He screams.

Sasha!

SASHA *comes to again.*

SASHA: Marcus, what on earth are you doing putting your hand in my plate? That's completely inappropriate, not to mention disgusting.

MARCUS: I'm sorry, I don't know what came over me.

SASHA: If you're still hungry, there's plenty left. You just have to ask.

MARCUS: I would like some more.

SASHA serves him another plateful. MARCUS dives in.

What is it?

SASHA: . . .

MARCUS: Is it a real recipe?

SASHA: . . .

MARCUS: Sasha!

SASHA turns to him again.

Is it a real recipe?

SASHA: What do you mean, a real recipe?

MARCUS: I don't know. I guess a real recipe is when you take time to measure all the ingredients. You smell it, add pepper, and cross your fingers that it will taste like happiness.

SASHA gets up from the table.

SASHA: I'm sorry, Marcus, but I have to get back to the zoo. If at least they still had some appetite . . . They don't eat, but they walk. A tragic journey. They have reserves of fat, true, but if they keep at it, they will quickly burn through the very last of those reserves.

. . .

SASHA starts to leave.

MARCUS: *(timidly)* Sasha . . . what you made for me . . . is it a real recipe?

SASHA: I don't understand what you're asking, Marcus. But if you're still hungry, don't be shy, help yourself.

MARCUS: I don't know what a real recipe is either. All I know is that . . . it's probably not throwing the spaghetti, tomatoes, AND the can in the pot of boiling water all at once while screaming, "I hate him, I hate him, I hate him!"

And then crying while stirring the pot.

Crying to the point of wanting to stick her own head in the pot, to turn into steam.

And finally, to faint, to be like dead while the spaghetti burns!

SASHA takes MARCUS in his arms.

SASHA: You are home here, Marcus. And tomorrow you will still be home here. And the tomorrow after that, and the one after that as well . . .

MARCUS: I have your word?

SASHA: Yes.

MARCUS: I'll put it in my pocket.

SASHA: I prepared this meal just for you, to welcome you. It's called fricassee. Veal fricassee. It's a real recipe.

MARCUS: That's a funny word.

SASHA: You think so?

MARCUS: Yes, "fricassee" sounds a bit funny.

SASHA: I gave that name to one of my bears. The female, the eldest, is called Fricassee. The director of the zoo was totally against it. He said that "Fricassee" was not a bear's name, that it sounded like "freak" or "messy," that it would tarnish the zoo's reputation. But I was set on calling her "Fricassee" because she was the first bear I took care of and fricassee is the dish I do best.

MARCUS: Have you been taking care of her for a long time?

SASHA: I fed Fricassee from a bottle. Today, she weighs two hundred kilos, if you can believe it. A monster . . . no, a goddess.

MARCUS: And the others, what are they called?

SASHA: I have three. The male's name is Goulash. We now have a baby, born in September, and his name is Couscous. Fricassee, Goulash, Couscous, three dishes I always get right. I was sure it would bring them luck.

. . .

MARCUS: It's . . . it's really delicious.

SASHA caresses MARCUS's head, then moves towards the exit. He changes his mind, comes back, kisses MARCUS on the forehead, and then leaves.

— 6 —

The zoo. The bears walk in the shadows. SASHA *continues moving the blocks of ice.*

SASHA's apartment. A bucketful of dirt has been spilt on the floor. Using a spoon, and with extreme meticulousness, MARCUS is filling small plastic bags with dirt.

SASHA enters, dragging his feet. He suddenly takes in the disaster area.

SASHA: I'm sorry, I must have the wrong apartment.

He exits. MARCUS keeps at it with much concentration. SASHA enters again.

I don't have the wrong apartment. That's unfortunate, because I wish I did have the wrong apartment. Because what I see here makes me want to scream . . . which is also a problem since I am too exhausted to scream. However, I will need to gather up my inner strength because while I do love the country and its vast expanses of wheat fields, what I love even more is going to visit it. I hate when it lets itself into my living room.

He yells.

Marcus, kindly explain the meaning of this crap!

SASHA lets himself drop to the floor, exhausted. MARCUS continues to work meticulously at his strange task.

MARCUS: It is not crap. I am not done, that is all. Once I'm done you won't be able to see a speck of dirt on the floor.

SASHA: Well, for now there's loads.

MARCUS: That's because I am not done.

SASHA: Might I know where all this dirt came from?

MARCUS: The gardens. The ones right next to the building. I got lucky: it's January, yet the ground isn't frozen. It didn't even take me a minute to fill the whole bucket.

SASHA: Would you mind explaining to me what possessed you to haul dirt from the gardens all the way to the apartment?

You are acting out because you are angry, is that it?

Because I promised to take the day off and go for a walk with you?

MARCUS: *(still busy)* . . .

SASHA: Marcus, I was up at dawn. You were still asleep. And even at that early hour, the temperature was so mild . . . I had no choice but to run over to the zoo to cool off my bears. It was obvious the temperature would only rise through the day.

. . .

Marcus, answer me: Is it because you're angry at me that you've covered the floor with dirt?

MARCUS: Not at all. I wanted to lighten your load.

SASHA: Oh, I feel much lighter for sure!

MARCUS: I thought of hot-air balloons.

SASHA: What?

MARCUS: When I woke up and saw that you couldn't take the day off, I said to myself, no problem, Marcus, you will put on your big boy pants and go for a walk by yourself. I went out of the building, took a few steps, and . . .

SASHA: And . . . ?

MARCUS: And the wind started to blow. I got scared that it would carry me away again.

SASHA: Marcus . . .

MARCUS: I got scared it would start tossing me around again at will, that it would start playing at knocking me against windows again. I got back to the entrance of the building in the nick of time. I saw the superintendent's bucket and that's when I thought of hot-air balloons . . . I know you don't have time to go for walks with me, Sasha, and I'm getting a little bored waiting for you all day. When hot-air balloons have their sandbags, the wind is powerless against them. I figured that bags of dirt would be the same . . . But I'm not sure whether it's better to make one big bag or lots of little bags. The hot-air balloons have lots, don't they? I think I'll hang a big one on each foot and lots of little ones around my waist . . . Like I said, it's not quite done. I still need to give it some thought.

SASHA: Marcus, come here for a second.

MARCUS: I can't, I'm working.

SASHA: Marcus, I am asking you to come here.

MARCUS: You're going to teach me a lesson? You want to give me a wallop I will remember all the way to my grave?

. . .

SASHA: Come here, please—I feel like having you close to me, that's all. You settle in whichever way you like. Does under my arm seem comfortable to you?

MARCUS gets closer. SASHA's arm is open, welcoming. MARCUS opts to sit down and snuggle in.

MARCUS: It's okay.

SASHA: For me too, it's okay.

Marcus, how can I say this . . . You came into my life at a very unusual time.

MARCUS: It wasn't the right time?

SASHA: I wouldn't put it like that.

MARCUS: I'm not an idiot, I could tell it wasn't the right time. You were waiting for winter and I showed up instead.

SASHA: I am waiting for winter. And for something else as well.

MARCUS: What?

SASHA: Another return.

MARCUS: That's why there's a date circled in red on the calendar?

SASHA: I am tired, Marcus. And not used to sharing my secrets. I need a little more time. But you have nothing to fear, little man.

— 8 —

SASHA's apartment. MARCUS is asleep. SASHA runs his fingers across the calendar.

SASHA: Two more weeks. Two more weeks until your return. That's too long, Anita. I can't stand your absence anymore . . . How I would have loved to be flamboyant in welcoming you. I fear you may find me rather worn out . . . What madness it is to try and replace winter . . .

9

A few days later. SASHA's *apartment. He enters, exhausted.*
MARCUS *is standing up straight, looking tense.*

SASHA: I can't feel my hands, can't stand my back . . . Thank good-
ness for coffee. They are predicting even higher temperatures? I
will roll with the punches. You'll see, Marcus, thanks to this coffee
pot, I will work at lightning speed.

MARCUS *doesn't react.*

Marcus, are you okay?

MARCUS *still doesn't react.*

You're allowed to speak, you know. Moving and talking are both
permitted here.

MARCUS: . . .

SASHA: People often call me strange, but you . . .

MARCUS: Don't say that! I am not strange!

SASHA: It's just a figure of speech, it doesn't mean anything.

MARCUS: Then why do you say it, if it has no meaning?

SASHA: Marcus, what's wrong?

. . .

MARCUS: A family of lizards in my belly. With all their cousins, too.

SASHA: That's pretty crowded.

MARCUS: It's because of tomorrow.

SASHA: School? That's tomorrow?

MARCUS: You forgot?

SASHA: No, no, not at all . . .

MARCUS: Did you buy all the supplies? From the list?

SASHA: Uh, yes, of course . . .

MARCUS: You did? Sasha, I was so scared of walking into class all naked-like. School started five months ago at least. Can you imagine going into the classroom, where you don't know anyone, no saliva in your mouth, and with an empty school bag on top of that . . . I would've died.

SASHA empties his bag onto the floor. He puts it across MARCUS's shoulder. He digs through the mess from the bag, pulls out a black pencil, and presents it ceremoniously to MARCUS.

SASHA: My little Marcus, you are now equipped to make it all the way to university.

MARCUS: I was under the impression the list was slightly longer than that.

SASHA: Nothing important, trust me.

MARCUS: Yes, but the box of coloured pencils was surely mandatory . . .

SASHA: Off to bed if you want to be ready for your big day.

MARCUS: Sasha . . . what if, tomorrow, the first assignment is to draw a picture?

SASHA: You can use your pencil.

MARCUS: And draw a picture in black and white? I'm too little for that. The teacher will think that I take myself very seriously.

SASHA: Would that be so bad?

MARCUS: Sasha . . . I'd like to go unnoticed. It's what I would like most in the whole world, to be like the others—so like the others that you couldn't tell us apart.

SASHA: You won't go unnoticed, Marcus. You'll be a new face. And they'll be pleased to see a new face. Stop worrying so much.

MARCUS tenses up again.

MARCUS: Sasha . . . if my bag is empty, I'll weigh next to nothing. The wind could take advantage of the fact that I'm walking to school . . .

SASHA: I promise you we will go to school hand in hand. The wind won't dare get near you. And now, come, it's time to sleep.

MARCUS: I'm not sleepy.

. . .

SASHA: What if I stayed with you tonight?

MARCUS: But the bears? You said we were headed for even higher temperatures . . .

SASHA: I owe you one.

MARCUS: What does that mean?

SASHA: Nothing. They'll understand.

SASHA's apartment, a few hours later. MARCUS is sleeping.
SASHA is working on equations in a notebook. Next to him,
a cup of coffee.

MARCUS: *(awaking abruptly)* Sasha! I dreamt I was suffocating, that my tongue went to hide at the back of my throat because the students in my class were asking what my nickname was. I couldn't answer, I didn't have one, and my tongue went to hide at the back of my throat forever! Sasha? Sasha?!

SASHA: I'm here, Marcus. Breathe. Please, just breathe.

MARCUS: Okay.

SASHA: But do it as well.

MARCUS breathes.

MARCUS: I can't go to school, Sasha. Everyone there must already have loads of nicknames.

SASHA: What are you talking about . . . It's normal for you not to have one. To get a nickname, you must first go to school. People must get to know you first.

MARCUS: I would really like for my nickname to be nice.

SASHA: It will be, it will be.

MARCUS gets back into bed. SASHA sits close by and goes back to his equations.

MARCUS: Aren't you going to sleep?

SASHA: I am trying to figure out how many more blocks of ice I will need to carry per hour. Three degrees higher, that's the forecast. I have to maintain a temperature that's bearable for my bears . . . though it's barely bearable . . . so to speak . . .

. . .

MARCUS: Sasha . . . the date that's circled in red on the calendar . . . what is it?

SASHA: Now's not the time, Marcus.

MARCUS: We know each other pretty well, now. Enough to share each other's secrets, don't you think? And I'm really curious about it.

SASHA: I'll tell you all about it tomorrow.

MARCUS: Actually, right at this moment, it's more the red pen you used to circle the date that makes me curious. That part of the story shouldn't be so long to tell . . .

SASHA smiles.

SASHA: Fair enough, I'll try and find your pen for you.

SASHA digs around. MARCUS is all hope.

Ah-ha!

MARCUS: You found it?

SASHA: Oh.

MARCUS: What?

SASHA: I forgot to put the cap back on. I'm sorry, Marcus.

MARCUS: *(undone)* It doesn't matter.

. . .

SASHA: Marcus, since you've been here, I know I haven't always stepped up. But if you could just wait another ten days . . . if you could just wait until that date that's circled on the calendar . . .

MARCUS: What's going to happen?

SASHA: In ten days, Anita will return. Anita is the love of my life. I promise everything will be better. Anita and I make one heck of a team.

MARCUS: You have a girlfriend?

SASHA: For the past seventeen years.

MARCUS: You've loved each other for seventeen years?

SASHA nods.

That's incredible . . . it must be a world record. Where is she?

SASHA: On a trip. A very long trip. Around the world.

MARCUS: Why didn't you go with her?

SASHA: I really would've loved to, as did she. It's a project we spent years planning. We chose every destination together . . . But at the last second I had to cancel. I realized . . . that I would never be able to be away from my bears. Not for that long.

MARCUS: She must've been angry with you . . . and with your bears.

SASHA: It was quite a disappointment for her, obviously. She was immensely sad, as was I. But we both knew I wouldn't enjoy the trip. That I might even ruin it for her. So we decided it was better for her to go alone, for her to live out our dream for both of us.

MARCUS: She's been gone a long time?

SASHA: Almost a year. In ten days it will be a year. She must already be in Norway—that was the last country on the itinerary. I'm the one who insisted a bit on that one, on ending the trip by going to see the bears of Norway.

MARCUS: Anita . . . was she happy to learn that I exist?

SASHA: I thought it best not to tell her anything prior to her return.

MARCUS: Oh . . .

SASHA: You have nothing to worry about, Marcus. Had she been by my side on that morning when you hit our window, she would've grabbed the ladder to go pick you like an apple even faster than I did.

MARCUS: Are you sure?

SASHA: Absolutely.

MARCUS: Then why didn't you say anything to her?

SASHA: I felt that learning over the phone that there was an extra little boy in her life might prove a shock. The phone is too brutal. Maybe I'm wrong . . . It isn't too late to tell her. What do you think?

MARCUS: I don't know . . . But in the end, I think that I think like you. It's likely quite rare for a lady to learn that she gave birth to a little boy while she was away. Best to go easy.

SASHA: She will love you, Marcus, believe me.

MARCUS: One Sasha and one Anita . . . it's almost too much. I mean, I may end up almost too normal . . .

This makes SASHA *laugh.*

— 11 —

The zoo. The bears continue their heavy march. SASHA puts blocks of ice down at their feet. MARCUS is at a distance, on the other side of the wire fencing.

MARCUS: It's as though I'm the one in a cage.

SASHA: No, it truly is them and I who are prisoners. And only winter will set us free.

MARCUS: Their fur is beautiful.

SASHA: Maybe. But under this fur, they are wasting away by the minute. Soon, I will be able to feel their bones.

MARCUS: Sasha . . . they won't die, will they?

SASHA: I will never let them die.

. . .

MARCUS: I had never seen real ones. I will have the best assignment of the class for sure. And no one will be able to copy me. Did I tell you that everyone started to draw in black and white?

SASHA: That's great. It's actually really, really great. You can start taking pictures, if you like. The camera's in the bag.

MARCUS: Not yet. I'll wait until they try to eat you.

SASHA: Sorry?

MARCUS: It'll make for more spectacular pictures when they try to eat you.

SASHA: Given their level of exhaustion, you might be waiting for a while.

MARCUS: But when they're healthy, they must want to devour you . . .

SASHA: Is that what you would do?

MARCUS: If I was a bear, I would try for sure.

SASHA: They know me too well. I've told you before, Marcus, what I feel, they feel. If they were to attack me, it would be like attacking themselves.

MARCUS: Well, I think that deep down they are not that wise.

SASHA: What do you mean?

MARCUS: That if they had another handler, they'd eat their hearts out.

SASHA: Me or someone else . . . What makes me so special?

MARCUS: Well . . .

He laughs.

You are a little strange.

SASHA: Oh, so you're using that word now . . .

MARCUS: Everyone says it at school.

SASHA: I thought as much.

MARCUS: Actually, I kind of like strange people. Maybe I'd even like to be strange, some day. But I think it's best to wait a bit. School really isn't the place for it. Yeah, if I really want to become strange, I'll wait until I am as old as you.

SASHA: That's your prerogative. But . . . might I know what makes me so strange?

MARCUS: Everything! Your work, your sleep . . .

SASHA: My sleep is linked to the bears' sleep, Marcus.

MARCUS: Actually, the strangest part is that, with you, I don't feel like doing stupid things.

SASHA *stops working.*

SASHA: Did you used to do a lot of stupid things?

MARCUS: I don't remember. I most likely never devoured anybody. But . . . maybe I've scribbled on a rug with molasses, maybe I've stolen some bicycles, maybe I even set fire to my bed once . . . I don't know. It's probably because I've hit my head on so many windows that I've lost my memory.

SASHA: You are allowed to forget.

MARCUS: Sometimes, when I'm at your place, my hands start to tingle. You know, like a really strong itch to do a stupid thing. A really stupid thing. But before I even have time to work out my plan, the tingling subsides. The itch is gone.

SASHA: And why is that?

MARCUS: Because you wouldn't notice.

SASHA: That's what you think.

MARCUS: Guaranteed: your head is always in the clouds. You see, there is no real pleasure in doing a stupid thing if no one is there to notice. I bet your bears think the same way.

SASHA: If they tried to devour me, I'm pretty sure I would notice.

MARCUS: Not so sure.

SASHA: You will get along great with Anita.

MARCUS: Why is that?

SASHA: "You've got your head in the clouds." She tells me that all the time.

MARCUS: Really? Maybe during her trip she will have found the exact cloud where your head keeps hiding . . .

    SASHA suddenly falters badly. Slowly, he makes his way to the ground.

Sasha . . . Sasha! Are you hurt?

SASHA: It's nothing. I just feel a little . . . light-headed.

MARCUS: You are whiter than the bears.

SASHA: In my bag, Marcus. There is a Thermos of coffee. Give it to me, please . . .

    MARCUS hands him the Thermos through the wire fencing. SASHA takes a sip directly from the Thermos.

MARCUS: Sasha, what's wrong with you?

SASHA: Nothing. I'm just tired.

MARCUS: You have to sleep more.

SASHA: I can't let my bears down.

MARCUS: But you don't eat either.

SASHA: I eat.

MARCUS: I've never seen you take a single bite. Sasha, you have to be as handsome as possible for Anita's return.

SASHA: You find me ugly?

MARCUS: No . . .

SASHA: Marcus, do you find me ugly?

MARCUS: No, it's just that . . .

SASHA: What?

MARCUS: I get the feeling that you wash less and less and that you have more and more hair.

SASHA smells himself, caresses his chin.

SASHA: It's true that I feel exhausted, Marcus. I'm afraid . . . I'm afraid I'll soon reach the end of my own reserves.

MARCUS: You know what I think?

SASHA: What?

MARCUS: That Anita's return will bring winter back.

SASHA: That's my hope as well.

MARCUS: But I have proof.

SASHA: What are you talking about . . .

MARCUS: You told me that you were both very sad on the day she left. I'm sure her eyes must have been blurry, so she couldn't have seen very clearly. She must have packed winter in her suitcase with the rest of her things, without noticing.

SASHA: I would like to believe that.

Marcus, would you like to come and join me?

MARCUS: You mean . . .

SASHA: Come through the wire fencing.

MARCUS: Go into the cage . . . with the bears?!

SASHA: You'll only get a chance like this once in your life. I wouldn't suggest it if they weren't so exhausted.

MARCUS: But, but, but . . .

SASHA: Don't be afraid.

MARCUS: What will they do to me?

SASHA: They'll look at you, nothing more. I'll tell you when to stop getting closer.

MARCUS: Me, Marcus, inside a bear cage? Are you sure they won't take advantage of the situation to eat their hearts out?

SASHA: I give you my word.

. . .

MARCUS: I'll put it in my pocket.

$$- \ 12 \ -$$

SASHA's apartment. His appearance is "rumpled," to say the least. He pours himself a cup of coffee, drinks.

MARCUS: Open the letter, Sasha.

SASHA: I'm sure that, once more, you're worrying about nothing.

He pours himself another cup, drinks.

Your teacher adores you.

MARCUS: Yes, but the teacher . . .

SASHA: She's likely writing to ask me for my fricassee recipe. That must be it, Marcus. Last week, no fewer than three parents of students from your class called me to ask for it. The lunches I pack for you appear to be quite a success.

Another cup.

MARCUS: Sasha, listen to me!

SASHA: I'm listening, Marcus. I'm listening.

MARCUS: The teacher gave me the letter at the end of the day.

SASHA: So?

MARCUS: This morning, it was my turn to present in front of the class.

SASHA: I'm certain it went well. Everybody loves bears.

MARCUS: Yes, but at the end, when I showed the picture, the one where I'm in the cage with the bears . . . the teacher asked me to come and talk to her in the hallway.

SASHA: What did she want?

MARCUS: She said . . . she was very worried. That she found it "irresponsible."

SASHA: Did you explain to her that this is my profession? That I know the bears better than I know myself?

MARCUS: Yes, but see, the teacher is terribly scared of dogs. When one comes to walk around in the schoolyard, she faints, every time. So it was a little difficult for her to understand that you and the bears are connected.

SASHA: Did she understand in the end?

MARCUS: I thought so, yes. But because of the letter, I'm not so sure anymore. Even though I repeated over and over how much care you take of them. That you were even working day and night because of the heat wave.

SASHA: You told her that?

MARCUS: But I also told her I didn't mind sleeping alone. I insisted on that.

SASHA knocks back one last coffee.

SASHA: Might be better to open it.

. . .

MARCUS: Is it bad?

SASHA: "I gather your situation is difficult. Perhaps together we might find a solution. I would invite you to come meet with me."

SASHA crumples the letter, throws it to the ground.

Who does she think she is?

MARCUS: She's nice, Sasha, I swear. She's worried, that's all.

SASHA: I know she's nice. But what does she know? What does she understand? Does she have a degree in bear sciences? I don't think so. Her letter is full of spelling mistakes.

MARCUS: She's just trying to help.

SASHA: I don't like it when someone feels entitled to sniff around in my life.

. . .

MARCUS: I like her a lot, Sasha. I would like you to meet with her. Even if just to reassure her.

SASHA: As though I had nothing better to do . . .

MARCUS: Did she suggest a date for the meeting?

SASHA: I didn't check.

MARCUS starts to wander in the apartment, seemingly nonchalant. In small increments he kicks the ball of paper in SASHA's direction . . . SASHA figures out the ploy, but also how important this is to MARCUS. Once the crumpled letter is within reach, SASHA grabs it, smooths it out.

It won't work.

MARCUS: Why?

SASHA: She suggests a meeting in three days. On the day of Anita's return.

MARCUS: You want me to suggest another day?

SASHA: Why do you insist I meet with her? After Anita's return, you nor anyone else will have anything to worry about anymore. If you want to reassure her, tell her that.

MARCUS: I will tell her.

The apartment. SASHA *and* MARCUS *are waiting at the door, side by side. Two hearts aflutter.* SASHA *is holding a large bouquet of flowers,* MARCUS *a smaller one.*

SASHA: What do you think of my hair?

MARCUS: Very clean.

SASHA: I meant the style.

MARCUS: Oh, sorry. Perfect.

SASHA: Does my jacket look too big?

MARCUS: I don't know, this is the first time I've seen you dressed like this. But it suits you.

SASHA: It's crazy how much weight I've lost recently. It must make me look older. Or no, in fact, maybe it makes me look younger.

MARCUS: What about me, do I look good?

SASHA: Of course.

MARCUS: Good enough to soften the blow?

SASHA laughs.

I don't see why that's funny. I know you better now—you're as nervous as I am.

. . .

SASHA: If you only knew, Marcus, how often I've dreamt of this moment. How many times I've counted the days on the calendar. I've missed Anìta so much. I still ask myself why I ever let her get into that cab.

Saying goodbye is such a strange thing to do. A hand that flutters in the void . . . Actually, no, the hand PUSHES BACK the void. The hand says, "Though you will be far, my love, there will be no void between us." That's what the hand is saying as it waves goodbye.

MARCUS: And how do you say welcome?

SASHA lifts MARCUS off the ground and spins him around.

SASHA: Like this! And again, and again!

MARCUS laughs heartily. Blackout.

* * *

An hour has passed. MARCUS *is sitting, eating.* SASHA *is still standing at the door, holding his bouquet. His eyes never completely look away from the door.*

MARCUS: I think this is your best batch of each of the three recipes.

SASHA: Marcus, make sure you leave room, eh?

MARCUS: I promise. I just want to fill the pit in my stomach.

SASHA: But look at the portions you've had! That's enough, now. You won't be hungry anymore. She'll be here any minute.

MARCUS: When there's fricassee, I always have enough room.

SASHA: Marcus, I want the three of us to eat TOGETHER.

MARCUS *pushes his plate aside and joins* SASHA, *waiting again, bouquet in hand.*

Her flight must've been a little delayed. That happens a lot.

MARCUS: Or maybe she encountered some problems at customs.

SASHA: What are you talking about? And first of all, what do you know of customs?

MARCUS: The mother of a boy in my class works at customs. He did his assignment about her. When you want to enter a country, the customs officers welcome you very politely, but, in fact, they are scrutinizing you from your eyebrows to your toes to make sure you are not a scoundrel. And that you don't have any cheese in your luggage.

SASHA: Anita doesn't like cheese. I'd be surprised if she took the risk of bringing some back.

MARCUS: Maybe, but . . . Can you picture the customs officer's face when he opened her suitcase, dug around a little, and found, hidden between her toothbrush and a pair of socks . . . winter?

SASHA laughs. Blackout.

* * *

SASHA is still waiting at the door. He is holding his bouquet in one hand, a cup of coffee in the other. MARCUS has collapsed at SASHA's feet, asleep, his little bouquet against his cheek. SASHA drinks more coffee, but his hand starts to shake, and then his whole body. He shakes more and more, to the point of dropping the cup. He takes his head in his hands.

Blackout.

— 14 —

The zoo. A few days later. SASHA *is not moving blocks of ice. He is walking in circles with the bears. His general state is pitiful.*

SASHA's apartment. MARCUS, his school bag on his back, is waiting for SASHA. SASHA enters.

MARCUS: Where were you? You were supposed to meet with my teacher this morning! You promised you would meet with her after all.

SASHA: I have but one meeting. One meeting . . . with Anita.

He crumbles to the floor. MARCUS makes a few desperate attempts to get him back up.

MARCUS: Get up, Sasha. Get up! Do you realize what's at stake if you don't show up for the meeting? Sasha, you really smell . . .

SASHA: I fell asleep in the bears' cage. I hadn't slept in so long . . .

MARCUS: You've got just enough time to wash up and put on your jacket. You promised me you would be as clean as a customs officer. Get up, Sasha, if you want us to remain a family.

SASHA: Marcus . . . Tell your teacher to go to hell.

MARCUS: She's only trying to help.

SASHA: If she agrees to go to hell, she'll find me there. She can then give me all the advice she wants. That's where I can be found, Marcus, nowhere else. Like in a nightmare, except it isn't a nightmare. It's my life. I'm in hell.

MARCUS: You can't say that.

SASHA: I would like to sleep, to sleep until eternity . . . It may be cowardly, but . . .

MARCUS is listening to SASHA, but for the past few seconds his gaze has been riveted on the window.

MARCUS: Sasha . . .

SASHA: Let me sleep, Marcus. Even if it is cowardly. I don't have the strength to cool off my bears anymore. And I don't have the strength to watch them exhaust themselves to death.

MARCUS: Sasha . . . please, look out the window.

It is snowing. SASHA finds the strength to get back up.

Snowflakes are falling by the thousands, Sasha. It's a real snowstorm. It's winter!

SASHA: My sweethearts, my furry darlings . . . At last, some peace. At last, some rest.

MARCUS: I bet Anita just went through customs!

SASHA: At last, sweet happiness.

SASHA holds MARCUS tightly in his arms. Together, in silence, they watch the storm's flurries.

The zoo. Despite the storm that blanketed the ground, the bears are still not sleeping. SASHA and MARCUS are wearing warm clothes.

MARCUS: It can't be right, Sasha, my cheeks are frozen. They should be sleeping.

SASHA: I don't understand.

MARCUS: Why aren't they sleeping?

SASHA: . . .

MARCUS: Sasha . . . What are we going to do?

SASHA: I don't know . . . All I know is that I can't take it anymore.

SASHA's *apartment. He is on a steady flow of coffee.*
MARCUS *enters.*

MARCUS: What are you doing here?

SASHA: I came to have dinner with you. I won't be able to stay
long, but . . .

MARCUS: Go back to your bears! Go brush them, rock them, whatever you want. No, what I wish is for them to eat you alive!

SASHA: Marcus . . . ?

MARCUS: The teacher and I waited for you for hours. Not to mention that she had been kind enough to reschedule the meeting
yet again.

SASHA: That was today? I'm so sorry . . . I'll send her some free
day passes for the zoo. She'll like that.

MARCUS: She couldn't care less about your bears! What she wants is to make sure you're taking care of me!

SASHA: Don't you like it here?

MARCUS: This might've been our last chance, Sasha! My teacher did everything she could to help us. And when a teacher senses she can do nothing more . . . that's always how it begins.

SASHA: How what begins?

MARCUS: That's when the wind starts to blow. To toss me around.

SASHA: Marcus . . .

MARCUS: I don't want the teacher to tell the principal. I don't want the principal to tell an inspector. I don't want an inspector to come and inspect you and decide to tear me away from you.

SASHA: That was never an option. I'm just asking you to be a little more patient. Soon Anita will be here . . .

MARCUS: No, Sasha.

SASHA: You'll see, when she gets here, everything will be fine.

MARCUS: She should have come home over a week ago, Sasha. January has come and gone. February starts tomorrow.

SASHA: It's because of winter. Her last destination was Norway. Given the storms we have here, imagine what it must be like in Norway. Obviously, the planes can't take off.

MARCUS: It's always because of winter . . . Take a look at yourself, Sasha.

SASHA: What's wrong with how I look?

MARCUS: Just look at yourself.

SASHA: Okay, true, I don't look like a customs officer. Well, good thing, really, because I am not one.

MARCUS: That's not the problem. The problem is that you are not even a Sasha anymore.

SASHA: Is that your teacher's idea? Did she put that idea in your head?

MARCUS searches through his bag and hands SASHA a box.

MARCUS: There are some leftovers if you're hungry.

SASHA: What is it?

MARCUS: My lunch for today.

SASHA: Why are you giving it to me?

MARCUS: Open it.

SASHA opens the box.

SASHA: . . . That's impossible . . .

MARCUS: The kibble you feed to the bears!

SASHA: I am sorry, Marcus. I must've been half-asleep. True, I prepared your lunch at the zoo, but I had everything with me . . .

MARCUS: The three classmates at my table saw the kibble. It made then want to vomit.

SASHA: Marcus . . . if you only knew how horrible I feel about this.

MARCUS: So now I do have a nickname: "bear breath." I even had to fight with my friends.

SASHA: Because they insulted you?

MARCUS: No. So they wouldn't tell the teacher. I was punished, but at least she doesn't know. If she had seen the kibble . . . you can be sure the wind would have started to blow immediately . . . For once I was doing good. I had a house, friends, I didn't have to be afraid of anything. And you're ruining it. Because of your bears. I'm sure that's why Anita doesn't want to come back . . . Because that's all that matters to you. Your damn bears!

MARCUS leaves the room.

SASHA: Marcus! Marcus, little man . . . I don't want to lose you.

SASHA goes to the calendar. He runs his fingers over it. He gathers his strength and tears away the page. He would like to have enough strength to crumple it, but that is still too painful.

— 18 —

SASHA's apartment. Night. MARCUS wakes up. He is calm.

MARCUS: Sasha, I dreamt I was making a bow. And arrows. Arrows with arrow-sharp arrowheads. I remember every detail from my dream. I remember exactly how to make arrows. Sasha? Sasha?

The zoo. The bears walk around heavily under SASHA's gaze. MARCUS enters, armed with a bow and arrow. SASHA observes him from a distance.

MARCUS: I'm sorry, bears. But I don't want to be thrown at windows again. I'm sorry, it's the only way.

He takes aim, ready to shoot. A red target appears on the bears' flanks. SASHA intervenes lovingly, without urgency.

SASHA: Marcus, please. Don't shoot.

MARCUS: I don't have a choice.

SASHA: You wouldn't even injure them . . . You would only hurt yourself.

MARCUS: I'm already hurt.

SASHA: Please, Marcus, drop your bow. I think . . . I know why the bears are not sleeping. It was never winter's fault. It was mine. That's what I came to tell them.

MARCUS puts down his bow.

MARCUS: What do you mean?

. . .

SASHA: Anita won't come back. I mean, she won't come back to live with me.

MARCUS: Did she call you?

SASHA: No . . . In fact, I haven't heard from her since she left.

MARCUS: You lied to me?

SASHA: I believed it, Marcus. I have never said a word to you I didn't believe. I needed to believe it, do you understand? I circled the date, closed my eyes, and believed it with all my might. I couldn't imagine that Anita would decide to leave me forever . . . Even if her leaving had been painful . . . She's obviously back in the country by now. But she hasn't contacted me in any way. I lost her, Marcus. I was incapable of travelling with her. I lost her.

. . .

MARCUS: Are you sad?

SASHA: Immensely sad. I never thought . . . it would be so heavy to bear. Heavier than ice. And the bears have been carrying this load for me until now.

It's not their burden, it's mine.

You know what? I think I'm an idiot.

MARCUS: I kind of like idiots . . .

SASHA: There are surely more storms ahead for me, Marcus.

MARCUS: I'm not afraid of storms anymore.

SASHA: I may not be the most pleasant person around. And, unlike you, I don't think I'm capable of healing in a day.

If the wind carries you away, Marcus, let yourself be carried away. Find a better window. I . . . I'm not a very good window. You deserve better . . . Do you need a lot of wind to fly away?

MARCUS: I don't know.

SASHA: I will blow. For your own good. I will blow, as hard as I can.

SASHA blows as softly as he can. Pfff . . .

MARCUS: Was that really . . . as hard as you can?

SASHA: I have nothing left in me.

MARCUS: I haven't moved a bit.

SASHA: Would you like me . . . to blow again?

MARCUS: Do you want to blow again?

SASHA: That's up to you. I will blow again . . . if you want me to blow again.

MARCUS: No. I want to live here, Sasha, with you.

SASHA wraps him up in his arms.

SASHA: My little man . . .

The bears start to yawn. They rub their backs on the ground, turn and turn again: slumber will be delightful.

SASHA & MARCUS: Oooohhh . . .

SASHA and MARCUS hold their breath . . . while the bears, one by one, fall asleep.

Blackout.

TRANSLATOR'S ACKNOWLEDGEMENTS

I would like to thank Geneviève Billette and the team at Playwrights Canada Press for trusting me with this ray of sunshine of a play. A special thank you goes to Blake Sproule, whose sensitive and careful copy-editing always turns that part of the process into a joyous correspondence. I wish to express my gratitude to the funding programs that support the sharing of our stories and voices across cultures through translation: we are blessed to have an opportunity to read and celebrate each other in this way. My admiration goes to Lynn Scurfield for the enchanting cover artwork that carries my imagination across artistic boundaries, translating the work anew. I would like to dedicate this translation to all the Marcuses who are still being tossed into windows by the wind: may you find your Sasha, settle under his arm, and put his words in your pocket.

Geneviève Billette holds a degree in French Studies from the University of Montreal and is a dramatist from the National Theatre School of Canada. She devotes herself to writing and translating and is a professor at the Graduate School of Theatre at the Université du Québec à Montréal (UQAM). *Le pays des mains*, published by Leméac in 2004, is the recipient of the Governor General's Literary Award, the Grand Prix Paul-Gilson, and the Prix Gratien-Gélinas. Her many plays have been performed in Switzerland, Canada, France, Martinique, Germany, and Mexico. Many have been translated into several languages. She lives in Montreal.

Translations by Nadine Desrochers include four plays by Sarah Berthiaume, two of which, *The Flood Thereafter* (Talisman Theatre, 2010) and *Yukonstyle* (Playwrights Canada Press, 2014), were part of Canadian Stage's 2013/2014 season; Marilyn Perreault's *Rock, Paper, Jackknife . . .* (Talisman Theatre, 2009; Playwrights Canada Press, 2010) and *BUS STOPS* (Théâtre I.N.K./Centaur Theatre, 2016); and *Billy (The Days of Howling)* by Fabien Cloutier (Talisman, 2014; A Play, A Pie and a Pint, Traverse Theatre/Òran Mór, Scotland). Her translation of *The Medea Effect* by Suzie Bastien (hotINK festival, New York, and Talisman Theatre, 2012) won the 2013 META Award for Outstanding New Translation.

First edition: November 2019
Printed and bound in Canada by Imprimerie Gauvin, Gatineau

Jacket art and design by Lynn Scurfield

**PLAYWRIGHTS
CANADA PRESS**

202-269 Richmond St. W.
Toronto, ON
M5V 1X1

416.703.0013
info@playwrightscanada.com
www.playwrightscanada.com
@playcanpress